Echoes from The Mountain

New and Selected Poems by
Mazisi Kunene

Malthouse African Poetry

Echoes from The Mountain

New and Selected Poems by
Mazisi Kunene

edited by
Dike Okoro

malthouse λ𝒫

Malthouse Press Limited

Lagos, Benin, Ibadan, Jos,Port-Harcourt, Zaria

Malthouse Press Limited
43 Onitana Street, Off Stadium Hotel Road
Off Western Avenue, Surulere, Lagos
E-mail: malthouse_press@yahoo.com
malthouse_lagos@yahoo.co.uk
Tel: +234 (01) -773 53 44; 0802 364 2402

Lagos, Benin, Ibadan, Jos, Port-Harcourt, Zaria

© Dike Okoro 2007
First Published 2007
ISBN 978 023 241 9

Acknowledgements

Acknowledgements are due to:
Africana Publishing Press, Heinemann (UK)
Kunene Family/Foundation
from which the selections have been made.

Many thanks to Mazisi Kunene and his wife, Mathabo Kunene, for welcoming and supporting this project. Thanks to Andries Botha, Janine, Sterling Plumpp, Sihawu Ngubane, Ntongela Masilela, and Lupenga Mphande, for reading, feedback, and support. I would also like to thank Reginald Gibbons and Tanure Ojaide for the encouragement. My family always - Kathy, Chuks, Phil, Omi, Obi, Ed, Pious, Pat, Bridget, Ogboronjo and Oke.

Four African Literatures: Xhosa, Sotho, Zulu, Amharic. Gerard, Albert.S. (University of California Press/Berkeley & Los Angeles, 1971) was an invaluable resource, as were:

Footnotes/extracts from the following books by Mazisi Kunene: *ZuluPoems* (1970), *Emperor Shaka* (1979), *Anthem of Decades* (1981), and *The Ancestors & the Sacred Mountains* (1982).

Thanks to Lupenga Mphande for the permission to use the cover photo.

Preface

This introduction, obviously long overdue, is unequivocally my utmost and sincerest thanks to the departed Mazisi Kunene and his most esteemed wife Mathabo, for believing in me and for letting me edit a wonderful work of art that attest to the prodigious dimensions and virtuoso of a fine poet. There is no doubt that a book of poems by Kunene is always a welcome addition to the circle of wordsmiths whose published collections define our lives and the conflicts that shape and beautify our world. Granted, no two writers write the same, which is why this book will certainly bring to readers far and wide the fine thoughts and vision of a legend in the arena of twentieth century African and world poetry. In very few instances I edited some areas, but I have left most of the poems in their original state because I want to show them to the public.

I have been deeply interested in Kunene's work since my first exposure to his visionary poems suffused with elements from the Zulu cultural matrix while still in my early teens in Port Harcourt, Nigeria. It would take me fourteen years later to finally meet the man I consider one of the most important voices of twentieth century African poetry/scholarship, be it in English or the indigenous African languages. Why a book by Kunene at this time? Although he has recently passed on, he has left behind a vacuum that can never be filled by a finer poet than him. Why should this book be read by every studious reader of quality poetry? How is this book going to advance or justify the legacy of South Africa's first ever poet laureate and his writings that helped shape and examine that country's glorious and always fascinating history?

The necessity of addressing these questions, *inter alia*, influenced the selection of poems in this book and helped to propel the commitment needed for the eventual publication of this book. But there is more to just the editorial aspect of this book. Nights and days spent at the desk alone, toiling through copies of Kunene's epics were not enough to sustain the project. In fact, this project built bridges between two generations, bridges cemented when Kunene and I finally met in his home in Durban, South Africa in June 2003. Right from that moment, we sparked a conversation threaded by a common appreciation for the arts, history, Africa, and the human condition. Our conversation, occasionally interrupted by laughs and pauses, often took us in circles around his work, for the man would rather discuss the accomplishments of his contemporaries from the continent and beyond rather than dwell on his illustrious career and numerous accolades and awards garnered. A modest gem, I concluded at the time. Kunene and I talked about Vilakazi, Soyinka, Achebe, Awoonor, Okigbo, Mqhayi and Okot and many others. Yet Kunene thought it important, without compromise, to remind me that B.W. Vilakazi, the renowned Zulu poet who wrote in English and Zulu language, produced a body of work he found most inspiring. As night fell while we sat in his back yard, I relayed to Kunene my intention to edit his work. "Go on, go on," he said, without hesitation. "That's work for your generation to do." Right there and then, I knew the conception of this book has been sanctioned. What was left was the commitment and persistence needed to materialize the idea. Too bad he had just left the hospital a few weeks back when we met and was rather unwell at the time of our meeting to carry on with a lengthy conversation. I therefore left early to afford him the time to get some rest as he got better by the days. My return to Chicago, USA was important then for two reasons. First, I had to complete and start off work on the anthology of Kunene's works right away. Second, I had to honor my research in Zulu literature made possible by a research grant from the USA/South African government.

I returned home in the US without saying goodbye to Kunene, even though he had encouraged me to see him before my departure. Time was of the essence. I wanted to get his published and unpublished works out there as soon as possible to honor a man who had just been rewarded for his contribution to the arts with the appointment as South Africa's first poet laureate, an honor which to me was long overdue. Kunene's four collections of poems published in English are still considered classics and major works of imaginative creation in African literature. His first collection, *Zulu poems*, proved to be an introduction to readers of African poetry and lovers of quality poetry beyond the continent, a reflection of a new, original, and important voice in African literature. African countries were still fighting for independence and grappling with the experience of severing ties with their colonial masters when he emerged as a published poet. Hence, as was the case then, many critics of African literature who reviewed and wrote criticism of the literature for the west and others developed an interest in the poetic expression adopted by some of Kunene's contemporaries from South Africa and other regions of the continent, with notable reference being the Ghanaian Kofi Awoonor, whose crafted poems were steeped in and modelled after traditional African poetic expressions/oral traditions. The German scholar Ulli Beier and his editorial partner Gerald Moore in their now classic penguin book of *Modern African Poetry* wrote,

> A few poets here, important in their influence if not Their numbers, have written extensively in their mother tongues and then translated their own work into English.The Ewe dirges of Kofi Awoonor, the Zulu poems of Mazisi Kunene and the energetic Luo songs of Okotp' Bitek are all examples of this indirect and often fruitful approach to the task of finding an acceptable

English 'voice' (20).

Beier and Moore's assertion here was highly critical and timely when it was first published for a good reason, as years later it served as a turning point for scholarly salvos and debates of works by Awoonor, Kunene, and p'Bitek. Consequently, Kunene's translated Zulu poems began to be viewed and recognized by his peers within and outside the continent as a significant contribution to the literary world.

In truth, Kunene's exploration of the cosmology and mythology of his Zulu heritage from a universal perspective is what defines the ethos of his opus. Much of his poetry is imbued with themes that touch on history, family, legacy, and the importance of the ancestors, worded in innovative language and steeped in vision that make his writing unique. In fact, in Kunene's poems one can easily recognize how the tripartite role of the artist as the custodian of Africa's heritage clearly unveils the singer, teacher, and leader as one. His poems, through language and images, show a connectedness between the present, past, and future. This is what we find in the poem "Ancient Bonds",

The strange shadows that nourish the bonds of our past
Greet us as we enter the dancing place.
They open the large wings of a cloud
Revealing a thin crescent of a rising moon.
The Ancestors invite us to the vision of the river
Knowing we have suffered enough;
Through them we float aimlessly on a dream
And yet our names must remain hidden from total joy
Lest through weakness we may succumb
Falling slowly into the depths of mindlessness.
Our love must survive through the ancient flames.
We must congregate here around the sitting mat,
To narrate endlessly the stories of distant worlds.

It is enough to do so,
To give our tale the grandeur of an ancient heritage
And then to clap our hands for those who are younger
than us.

This poem speaks to a vision beyond the arts. Kunene's importance in the idea of nation building can be easily seen as a fructifier in this poem. As a writer who once represented the African National Congress in Europe and the USA before embarking on a long and fruitful teaching career, one can reasonably conclude that his poems are conscious attempts to recapture and place history in its appropriate context. And he has thus served his time in that regard, despite the nightmares he and many writers suffered under apartheid.

Kunene's departure from South Africa to Europe and later the US following the ruthless regime of apartheid also has underpinnings and relevance to his later poems which, for the most part, dealt with family and bonds with relatives. My favorite recollection of his poems here would be "A Vision of Zosukuma", where he talks with such glaring passion, authenticity and charm about his son. This poem affirms the importance of not just fatherhood but parenthood as benchmark for the continuation of a legacy.

With the courage of the sea
I charged into the shores of the earth,
At the end of the white mist
A face, my child, a face of the beautiful sun,
Travellers wait for him.
They come from the four directions of the earth,
From this centre there is a winding path,
Long stems of flowers hang over the earth,
They swell with the seed of the new year.
My child takes the poem that is old
And learns from it our own legends
To see life with the eyes of the Forefathers.

For all creatures have their way of finding a
home,
Like the hunting dog, like the stampeding
elephant,
Like us who have found a moving mountain.

Strong images, memorable similes, and powerful
metaphors sustain the strength of this poem and carry the
message through. Kunene is once again at his best,
meshing vision with the precision of a seasoned craftsman.
Lines 1 and 2 establish the journey of fatherhood as he
works to build a legacy: "With the courage of the sea/I
charge into the shores of the earth." This commitment of
exploration is tied to the setting of a foundation. And
that's what we find when he unveils the result of his search
in line 3-5: "At the end of the white mist/A face, my child,
a face of the beautiful sun/Travelers wait for him." The
rest of the lines weave a learning process for the child, and
we are once again reminded by Kunene of the importance
of seeing children as the inheritors of legacies established
by the ancestors. In the end, his voice justifies his
composition, making him a poet conscious of the
importance of nature to humans, and how the joy of
childbirth transforms a parent. So that the success of his
poetry, as we have come to know, lies not in mere
recollection of events, but in meshing images and stories
with a language that gives originality and depth to his
verse. His poetry leaves the reader with what Chinua
Achebe once stated when asked to explain his citation of
Kunene's book of epic poems *Emperor Shaka* towards the
end of his novel *Anthills of the Savannah* that 'as Africans
today we should make it a habit of invoking these powerful
images from our history, legend and art...You don't have
to repeat everything that Kunene said, but just mention the
keyword, the password, and the whole image is called up in
the imagination of those who know, who are aware, who
are literate in our traditions. I think this is very important."

Achebe's conclusion then brings to mind the role of the poet/artist as singer, teacher, and leader of thought.

Despite the often, necessary need to be aware of the mythological allusions that abound in Kunene's poems, it is clear that his poetry is written with an ear for sound and a philosophical outlook on life. Kunene's poems, often epics and lyrics, represent a tradition similar to the poems of Aime Cesaire, Derek Walcott, and the great Xhosa poet Samuel Mqhayi and the great nineteenth century poet Mshongweni. They tell stories, and from these stories we learn new things about the poet's vision and how it is informed by the need to celebrate life and its complex realities. This is what makes the poems in this collection a befitting memory of the fine poet and a formal introduction of his works and creative hindsight to the American readership. And, like most of Kunene's poems, the poems herein collected were not selected in any form to show the very best of his works, but were selected on the basis of simplicity in form and accessibility to audience. A poem by Kunene that I believe conveys a simplicity in thought while depicting the imagery of survival is the moving and passionate "Peace", which evokes the history of unrest in black townships and also symbolizes all that happened elsewhere on the continent,

> Sing again the great song,
> Sing it with the winds that are shaking the reeds.
> Sing until the whole earth is shaken by the song.
> Maybe summer may yet come again.
> They summon you, who stand at the ruins.
> They praise your once great kingdom,
> Teeming with free men.
> Over there, in the villages devastated by war, they are calling
> Saying: 'Come you who broke the battle axe,
> Men are cutting men on the river bed.'
> The waters that ran with the rainbow
> Are curled with clots of blood;

The new seedlings sprout no more.
But you who speak with a dream
You will visit us
And unveil the new age
Letting us sleep on our backs
Listening to the multitudes of the stars.

The brilliance of this poem lies in the execution of imagery that doesn't bore the reader with details. Each line has a strong image, and each image performs a function that elevates the message intended by the poet. Kunene has not forgotten the past and recalls it with nostalgia and hope, even when things do not seem to be right. He declares, "Sing again the great song/sing it with the winds that are shaking the reeds/sing until the whole earth is shaken by the song." The thought here is revolutionary. Change comes with protest/action. And hope springs from the hearts of those who believe in change. South Africa's apartheid past is revisited here. And those who believe in change are the people called upon or invoked rather, as Kunene sings, "But you who speak with a dream/you will visit us/and unveil the new age." The sense of a new beginning and phase is present in his vision. This is what separates Kunene from other poets of his generation. That ability to philosophize conflicts and provide a probable solution, are special characteristics of his writing style and attempt at examining the ironies of life.

Many people were very supportive of this book and encouraged me along the way. I am personally grateful to Reginald Gibbons, Ntongela Masilela, Tanure Ojaide, Lupenga Mphande, and Sihawu Ngubane for their encouragement. I would also like to use this medium to thank Mathabo Kunene and the Kunene Foundation for believing in this pivotal work of literature, art, and history.

Dike Okoro, *Chicago, 2007*

Contents

I

Zulu Poems
(1970)

Triumph of thought

So I put thoughts on the palm of your hand
And let the pleiades race in the sky;
Winter will try again to overwhelm us
But we shall be ready with the warmth of blood.
And you, in the company of twins, will shelter us.
Then she, the widowed leopard, will retreat into the hill
And there howl all night long.
She will walk about naked and destitute
Deprived of the glory of her victims.
You alone will triumph in your power.
The male calf will find its joy in the stampede
Beating the ground with its triumphant hoofs
Because it shall be the young bull of the earth.

Place of dreams

There is a place
Where the dream is dreaming us,
We who are the shepherds of the stars.
Its stands towering as tall as the mountains
Spreading its fire over the sun
Until when we take one great stride
We speed with the eagle on our journey.
It is the eagle that plays its wings on our paths,
Wakening another blind dream.
Together with other generations hereafter
They shall dream them like us.
When they wake on their journeys they will say:
Someone, somewhere, is dreaming us, in the ruins.

Time will come

Time will come
Bringing the gifts of her secrets.
These arms that are bound into infinity
Will kindle the flame of the volcano
Erupting with light onto our paths.
Imagination shall overpower the children of the sun
Making them burst forth with our tomorrows.
They shall give birth before their innocence has been
consumed.

A farewell

I who have sung you songs over the years,
I depart.
The staff is broken
The young ebony plant sinks in the mud.
These winds are wailing with seeds.
They will scatter them on the open space
Where rains will give birth to jungles.
I believe in the great day
Which will make our paths meet:
I shall wake then from the desert
Seeing you approach with pots filled with water.
We shall sit at the place of the old man
Untying the knots in the expanse of the afternoon,
In the fertility of the fig tree,
In the vastness of the willow tree,
In the savannahs of the fleeting antelope.

When I looked back

I am haunted by your nostalgia,
You who reaped the flesh,
You whose paths cry with pain,
You who have power over the skulls of the earth.
I miss you even in the night of barren women,
I wait in vain for your shadow.
When I find it intertwined in my fingers
I open the door eagerly
Thinking you may emerge.
I search for you in the piles of the dead.
I do not find you.
This great nostalgia
Attacks me in the midst of bats.
I rushed like a wounded bird until I was silent
Under the buildings of those greater than you.
Perhaps it was my ghost fears
That made you tower above me.
Perhaps I was in the company of inferior men.

Thoughts on June 26*

Was I wrong when I thought
All shall be avenged?
Was I wrong when I thought
The rope of iron holding the neck of young bulls
Shall be avenged?
Was I wrong when I thought
The orphans of sulphur shall rise
From the ocean?
Was I depraved when I thought there need not be love,
There need not be forgiveness, there need not be progress,
There need not be goodness on the earth,
There need not be towns of skeletons,
Sending messages of elephants to the moon?
Was I wrong to laugh asphyxiated ecstasy
When the sea rose like quicklime,
When the ashes on ashes were blown by the wind,
When the infant sword was left alone on the hill top?
Was I wrong to erect a monument of blood?
Was I wrong to avenge the pillage of Caesar?
Was I wrong? Was I wrong?
Was I wrong to ignite the earth
And dance above the stars
Watching Europe burn with its civilization of fire,
Watching America disintegrate with its gods of steel,
Watching the persecutors of mankind turn into dust.
Was I wrong? Was I wrong?

---

* South African Freedom Day

Presence

Sleep tries to split us apart
But dreams come and open our gates.
You descend with the sound of bells
And enter into the center of a large house,
Playing with wild dogs.
I tear off the doors from the east
And throw them into a great fire
Where they burn and light your face.
It is beautiful like a vast planet.
Your face turns as if to smile
But a distant voice calls you back
And you disappear without talking,
Leaving the nostalgia of your image.

Nozizwe*

You were to be the center of our dream
To give life to all that is abandoned.
You were to heal the wound,
To restore the bones that were broken.
But you betrayed us!
You chose a lover from the enemy,
You paraded him before us like a sin,
You dared embrace the killer of your father,
You led your clans to the gallows,
You mocked the gods of our Forefathers,
You shouted our secrets before the little strangers,
You mocked the sacred heads of our elders,
You parleyed their grey hair before the children.
Their lips that hold the ancient truths were sealed.
By their sunken eyes your body was cursed.
The moving river shall swallow it!

---

* A traitor who served the South African Police

8

Abundance

I possess a thousand thundering voices
With which I call you from the place of the sinking sun.
I call you from the shaking of branches
Where they dance with the tail of the wind.
You are the endless abundance
Singing with the lips of all generations.
You are like a trunk lush with branches in the lake
Whom the feller of woods felled in vain,
But sprouts with new buds in summer.
When it is loaded with fruit he comes again
And eats to satiation desiring to end its season;
But again and again the branches shoot forth with new
seasons.

In memory of a fanatic

Almost a thousand years ago.
Your tears are dry on a stone,
Your perfumes are commingled with dust.
What was the use of this death?
Those who saw your gigantic arm across the skies
Spreading the inscriptions of faith
Were the locusts on the dry fields of maize
Who let their wings flutter from age to age,
Who carried the fire with their lips,
Singeing your long hair in the wind.
They bent their faith according to the times.

A poem

May I when I awake take
From all men
The yearnings of their souls
And turn them into the fountain of Mpindelela[*]
Which will explode into oceans;
Not those of the south that are full of bitterness
But those that are sweet to taste.

---

[*] Kunene's explanation of the significance proper names in Zulu poetry (Quote taken from the introduction to poetry collection, Zulu Poems-- 1970): "Proper names in Zulu poetry are sometimes used as a literary device. In such cases they do not necessarily refer to a real person, but are part of a system of ideas or personifications...Here we can assume firstly that there is such a fountain (ideally there ought to be) or secondly, that the name Mpindelela-'recurrent' –is descriptive of recurrent yearnings, or thirdly, that the name describes the action of the fountain. The apparent meaning, namely a desire to drink and rest with others at the fountain of Mpindelela, must be as intense and satisfying as if this was the only meaning possible in the poem. On the other hand, if we have understood the poem in its metaphorical sense, the concept of the fountain is extended in its meaning by the name Mpindelela. The dual levels of meaning often interact, share the verbal meanings and implications" (21-22).

Peace

Sing again the great song,
Sing it with the winds that are shaking the reeds.
Sing until the whole earth is shaken by the song.
Perhaps summer may yet come again.
They summon you, who stand at the ruins.
They praise your once great kingdom,
Teeming with free men.
Over there, in the villages devastated by war, they are calling,
Saying: 'Come you who broke the battle axe,
Men are cutting men on the river bed.'
The waters that ran with the rainbow
Are curled with clots of blood;
The new seedlings sprout no more.
But you who speak with a dream,
You will visit us
And unveil the new age,
Letting us sleep on our backs
Listening to the multitudes of the stars.

Man

May I divorce myself from philosophers
Who stand detached from the affairs of men,
Who turn their hearts into clay.
I had met men I despised
But it was they who made the cauldron of the earth,
Alone raised the star,
Surpassing the glory of the sun.

Others

When I have fulfilled my desires
Let me take these grain baskets,

And fill them up with other men's desires,
So that whoever crosses the desert
May never starve.

Friends

Honey are the words you speak
Whilst I drift slowly into sleep.
You tell the story over and over again.
I drowse in the palm of your hand
Whilst you hold the body aching with pain.
Softly you cover it and whisper
in my ear.
Although knowing I do not hear you,
You do it for the heart
Which alone never sleeps.

On the death of young guerillas

You called me, but I made no response in that night;
I feared you, you whose power strikes with terror.
You killed my children with a blunt spear,
You held me back so that I may not bury them.
The soil disgorges them:
Wherever I go I find their bodies scattered.
Could it be that you are tired of the old ones
Who reappear in the valley of dreams?
Could it be they whet your appetite with their flesh?
Could it be you are blind in your destruction?

The power of creativity

The sea echoes in the caves
Celebrating its conquest into the darkness,
Exploding from the belly of the earth
Until the giant bulls are awakened from their sleep.
They cry till their voices split the moon.
Blood flows into the blanket of the skies
Congealing into coils of mist.
Your power struts on the cliffs like a gorilla.
You return having conquered the earth.
I know, because dawn advances,
You will never be conquered by cowards.
You will break their fortress
Releasing the leaf that has long been buried,
Making it quiver on the shore of great waves,
Kindling the lips that have long been silent.

To the watcher of the gates

Watcher of the gates of life,
Let me enter with my children
To sing within great anthems.
We have long promised, on the wings of the eagle,
That we shall break open the skies
And release the wild horses of heaven.
They will dance and run in the wide east,
While we with our dreams hold onto them
Until we arrive at the end of the world.
We shall enter a million great villages
And tell those within great tales;
They will not again awake with grief,
But will emerge with the rays of the sun
Playing to us their songs.
Alas! It is you, mother of Nomavimbela, who holds us back,
You make us uncertain with your long shadows.
When we have merged
We shall create one world, a world full of epics.

The civilization of iron

I saw those whose heads were shaved,
Whose fingers were sharpened, who wore shoes,
Whose eyes stared with coins.
I saw them
In their long processions
Rushing to worship images of steel:
They crushed the intestines of children
Until their tongues fell out.
I saw iron with sharp hands
Embracing infants in the flames.
They wandered on the roads
Preaching the religion of iron,
Pregnant with those of blood and milk.
I saw milk flowing
Like rivers under the feet of iron.
The earth shrank
And wailed the wail of machines.
There were no more people,
There were no more women,
Love was for sale in the wide streets
Spilling from bottles like gold dust.
They bought it for the festival of iron.
Those who dug it
Curled on the stones
Where they died in the whirlwind.
I saw the worshippers of iron
Who do not speak.

II

Emperor Shaka (1979)

Dedicated to all the heroes and heroines of the African continent and all her children who shall make her name great

Dirge of the palm race

The great cloud opens: the mountain has fallen.
Silence hangs on to the shoulders of the heavens.
The thunderbolts travel making the skies tremble.
The flashes of lightning haunt our earth with destruction.
'The mountain has fallen, the earth's center quivers.'
Great Protectors, Beautiful Ones, Forefathers, come!
Run into the semi-circle of the wind and carry the child.
Take him with both arms and utter these words:
'It is we who planted the sacred word,
It is we who accompany you into the night.
We have summoned you with our songs and epics.
Our home awaits you with an eternal feast.
All Beautiful Ones have begun to sing their anthem'.
Our nation is like the wind – it will go on and on forever!

Great ocean, throw the white wave
And let the feet of the hero be seen on the sand.
Through the mirror of the silent lake
Let us see the eyes of the Forefathers.
Let us watch the Ancestors with their children.
Let the generations hereafter say in their song:
'It is not I alone who was chosen by the gods.
The children of the Palm Race multiply.
In the eternal spring there is the song of the morning.'
Here is the mountain of Ngoye, Son of Gumede,
It is rising to touch the sky
And the lips of generations speak in her womb,

For whatever we do in the name of the Forefathers is
eternal.
The whirlwinds shall not uproot it from the ground
Until we enter the center of the earth...
Nandi, daughter of Bhebhe, is it you who approaches?
Touch then the wound with your fingers,
Tell my child he must listen to you,
He must listen to the Ancestors as they sing the song.
Here they come! Dingiswayo, son of Jobe: 'Bayede!'
Mbikwane, voice of the gentle rain: 'Bayede!'
Mghobhozi, brother of the sacred mountain: 'Bayede!'
The Ancestors are bringing the emblem of the black beads.

At the grounds of Bulawayo people are frightened of the
night.
Shaka! They are shouting your name, they are calling you,
Their hands are heavy like iron on their heads:
'The mountain has fallen, the earth trembles.'
The wind carries the voices of the women
The wound is tended by women, the wound is dark.
'Our child is dead, our sun breathes the final agony.'
Have you ever heard the wailing voices of women?
The women came first before us!
The women tell us when our calabash shall be swallowed
by the night,
The women hear first the crying of the infant.
'Our child is dead, the Ancestors have come.'
They summon the rain, they speak through the opening:
'We have arrived. We have come to take the child.
Whoever was last to speak against him shall follow us,
He shall be judged among the Forefathers;
They shall tie him with a rope and bury him!'

They know best, they were here at the beginning of time.

They saw the procession of elephants to the mountain.
We must do their bidding and put the stone on the cairn,
We must raise the grain basket and scatter the seeds.
Summer will come and envelop the earth.
When all the enemies have died
And their bodies are reeked through with worms,
Those who are born from his plant shall honor him!
They shall fill the gourd with water to make the sacred
mark.
They shall arrive at the feast at the crack of dawn,
They shall listen to the epics of the Forefathers.
Because they are older than our children
They shall ask them to tell us the truth:
'After the Mourning-of-the-Circling-Vultures
There shall be the Feast of Return.
Your children shall dance on the ancient grounds.
The earth itself shall yield, opening its lakes,
People shall drink and sing the song.'

Great Ancestral Forefathers, because you are older than
we are
Accompany us into the night,
Tell us the tale while our trembling eyes follow the path;
Let us learn to speak the language of poets.

Beautiful Ones! Restless-feet-feet-of-the-morning, come!
Touch our shoulders and wake the ram from sleep;
Give us the courage of the river.

He who is like an Ancestral Spirit cannot be stabbed.

He is like the stars of the Milky Way as they climb the heavens.
He is like the rain that falls on the heads of the ripening plants.
He is the forest that keeps secret our legends.

He is an Ancestral Spirit; he cannot be stabbed.
Even now they sing his song. They call his name.
They dance in the arena listening to the echoes of his epics
Till the end of time – they shall sing of him.
Till the end of time his shield shall shelter the hero from the winds,
And his children shall rise like locusts.
They shall scatter the dust of our enemies,
They shall make our earth free for the Palm Race.

Ngoye: mountain
Bayede: was originally 'Bayethe' meaning 'bring them (the enemies), we are ready to fight them.'
Jobe: father of Dingiswayo and King of the Mthethwas
Dingiswayo: King of the Mthethwas and founder of the Mthethwa empire
Shaka: founder of the Zulu nation
Nandi: daughter of Bhebhe and mother of Shaka
Mbikwane: Paternal uncle of king Dingiswayo. A highly respected political figure, he was made governor by Shaka over the white coastal settlement
Bulawayo: signifies Shaka's harem and regiment
Mghobhozi: reference here is to Mghobhozi of the Msane clan
Gumede: mythic figure associated with the mountains

III

Anthem of decades (1981)

Dedicated to
Goddess Nomkhubulwane, Goddess Maat
Nandi of the Zulus (mother of Shaka)
Yaa Asantewa, Kahina, Candace
Mkabayi (female founder of the Zulu nation)
Ranavala, Labotsibeni
Maqandeyana (the philosopher)
Yimama (the teacher)
all the great women of the African continent
and their children

Anthem of decades (extract from an epic)

Part I

And then time was born:
The millipede-darkness encircled the earth
And silence surged into space like a pregnant moon.
Tufts of darkness entangled in the horizon
Making the earth heave like a giant heart.
The crooked mountains await the first fruit of the sun.
While the night triumphed, the stars thrust their swords of light,

(Which, the tale goes, were words older than ours)
Tearing the black blanket with its hidden mysteries.
The creator who created heaven and earth
Filled this planet with the commotion of beasts
And walked the great path of skies,
Looking on the hungry chasms of the mountains,
The racing of great rivers and spacious oceans
Whose waves beat eternally on the vast shores.

The belly of the earth split open
Releasing animals that crawl on the earth
And others that fly with their wings
And others that drum their hoofs on the ground.
The lion roared thundering the first fear.
Other beasts less ferocious stared

Until, aware of the satisfying taste of blood,
They joined in the general carnage.
So the lesson was learnt. Life must continue
And good things must feed the ruthlessness of appetites.

At the beginning the creator had messengers
Whom he sent to the ends of the universe:
Sodume, the Intelligence of Heaven,
Who explored the labyrinths of the earth
And opened the gates to all the creatures that inhabit the
earth.

Satisfied with this work
He sang as they paraded:
'These multitudes will fill this world of stone,
The forests will be stampeding with wild animals,
The mountains will be gamboling with antelopes,
The overflowing rivers will be pregnant with life.
But in all this man is yet to come,
Proud and defiant before all things.'
So over and over he repeated the ecstasy of heaven
Like him who sings alone the anthems of life.

There was Simo who stood guard
At the limits of the universe,
Who blotted out, at intervals, the light of the moon
And darkness would return to the earth hoping to regain
its lost territory.
He travelled often accompanied by the children of
Sodume,
The wild ones who loved best
To flash the forks of lightning.

Their father Sodume lived near the earth
Where he played games with his wife Nodume.
She screamed, echoing her voice across the path of the sky.
But Sodume's voice, round and powerful, shook the
heavens.
Often he emerged with her in relentless pursuit.
Both cherished the blue bird of heaven
Whose tail was deep blue, whose wings were blue,
Whose body was blue but whose feet were of burning red.
Wherever they were they let it fly before them like a cloud.

Sometimes it would spread its wings, descending on the
earth
And tearing firm mountains from their roots.
Those who know say even its lungs spit fire
Whose great flames shatter the earth
So that in the minds of all
It symbolized the wrath of the gods.

In all this the power of the creator
Revealed itself in his daughter, the princess of life,
Nomkhubulwane.
She was the source of all life.
She gave abundance to the hungry of the earth.
For this even animals hailed her in their worlds
And gamboled like young calves at play.

The princess of life was loved for her songs,
Whoever heard them would lie down
Repeating their music over and over again in his heart.
Even on this day of august debates
They all listened as she touched on the unknown and

beautiful themes,
Saying: 'We have fulfilled the other tasks of creation
But they are not complete without man,
He who will bind all things of existence,
A great shepherd who excels with wisdom.'
She did not indulge in long endless debates
Since even those who listened to her took long to understand
As on the day of creation they did not understand.
But Somazwi, dreaded by all, who speaks with the vehemence of fire,
Did not wait long, like all who are poised with suspicion,
Terrified of the power that challenges them in their glory,
They who follow all new ideas with the violence of their eyes.
He replied like one whose words burn the lips
And said: 'Here begins again the old tale of blunders
As when long ago we remonstrated in the wind,
Saying it is enough that our great assembly exists,
We, the ultimate expression of the power of the creator.
But now we hear this strange story of a new power
That will supervise all things with knowledge.'
He spoke as they all listened with extended ears
Knowing that though they did not hold affection for him
His mind was as swift as the horn of a bull.
His followers clustered together like a brood,
As always, applauding each word he put forward.
Others delighted in the clash of words
Saying let the giants show their strength.
They waited for Sodume,
Whose intelligence baffled those known for their wisdom
As if even the winds listened when he spoke.

Somazwi continued: 'What will this creature do
With knowledge that excels all created things
Endowed as they are with enough for each day.
On the next day they still have enough for their daily needs
But I fear that this creature on knowing so much

Will experience the pains of yesterday and the unfulfilled
tomorrow.
When it realizes the defects of its clan
It will build dreams that will never be fulfilled
And wander everywhere with painful doubts asking the
question
"What is the earth, of what value is life?"

It will not be enough to revel in the beauties of an earthly
life.'
He spoke so wisely that even those who supported
Nomkhubulwane
Began to doubt and were swayed by Somazwi's thoughts.
All shook in their seats with questions.
Sodume alone listened
As if inspired by visions others could not reach.
He turned to his wife, who rested her hand on his
shoulder,
Saying: 'The life we live deprives us of wisdom,
We are overwhelmed by things before us.'
Scarcely had he finished these words when someone stood
Turning to him as if he heard him:
'Great fighter who overwhelms with fierce powers
Do not allow the fire of words to burn beautiful things
As if these words were the very kernel of truth.
Unsheath your thoughts and cut these poisonous doubts

Of even those who have been swayed.
We all know a great path leads forward.
In it, all solutions evolve.
You, with only a few words, can straighten crooked
thoughts.'
He was silent and so were all the others.
It was as if whoever spoke first would create great
conflagrations.
Sodume did not respond.
He listened like all wise men
Who do not rush without untying each knot.
Sometimes when they discover the truth they only laugh in
their hearts
Knowing how words are like seeds
Which fall from the hands in their hundreds, most dying in
their shells.
One who was known for his love of pleasure stood up
And thought he might speak.
So that they may remember pots frothing with beer
He said: 'How can we solve in a day such great mysteries
We must settle down under the shade, delving into the
truth.'
Others stared at each other, pleased with these words
But none was eager to be seen filled with enthusiasm

Since there must be no talk of hunger in great assemblies.
Opponents continued to talk fiercely,
Saying: 'The creation of man is no desire of the creator.'
It seemed those who opposed the creation of man would
triumph,
Bidding with their words saying:
'This foolish creature will walk blindly, knowing and yet

not knowing.
Since a pleasant life must define its boundaries.'
After a long debate
Nomkhubulwane was heard asking for their attention.
She called over and over again, as she had provoked the debate.
As she stood up the sun shook with her shadow.
Addressing him who favored beasts to man,
She said: 'These arguments of the day have strange forebodings.
Those who oppose the hand of creation
Do so believing that what is, is complete.
But they do not understand, creation must always create.
Its essence is its change.
Form, its abundance, splits itself to make abundance.
Whoever loves its greatness does not question it
Since to question is to weave strange tangles.
Its greatness is its expanse as always.
Somazwi and all those who are swept by his words do not know
That this creature, man, shall derive his power
From the very struggle of incomplete power
Which alone will rouse his mind with the appetite for wisdom.'
She spoke these words knowing what lay hidden in their fears.
Even now the truth of what was to come formed itself within them.
They all listened, even the excitable followers of Somazwi,
Since they still held her high in their esteem not for prestige,
But for her thoughts that burn like a thin sword.

He who had long depended on wisdom for his fame called
out.
As he began to talk they all turned their eyes,
Guessing what wisdom Sodume was to unravel.
'I have listened to the skilful tongues
Saying what value will it be to man
That he should walk in ignorance, blind of his fate.
But such questions and remarks have their weaknesses.
Whoever is the umbilical cord of life denies his existence
If he disputes the oneness of which he is extension.
It is not he alone who is, who is the reality of creation,
But those who are and others who shall be,
Since the eye of life extends to the vastness of eternity.

The daughter of heaven has spoken all truths.
Whoever has not heard
Harbours his own kind of truth which he shall not reveal
before us.'

The great gathering listened,
Each trying to untie the profound meanings in Sodume's
words.
Some questioned these thoughts, saying truth is always
relative,
But others could not reach conclusions,
Their faces rigid with amazement.
Sodume continued: 'The mind is the essence of conquest.
If man is endowed with this power,
Even lions who boast of their strength will fear him.
I and others who love the extension of life
Say let men stand supreme over the earth.'

The chorus of those who agreed echoed
And as was customary a great anthem was heard,
A eulogy from those who favored mankind.
Someone from the assembly shouted:
'It is ours, this voice, it is ours.'
When this mysterious debate was over, they all dispersed
in their ways.
There were great feasts at the house of Somahle,
Who was the source of all pleasure;
Whoever entered this house reveled as he wished.
A great hubbub was heard as they laughed and drank.
Some held beer pots decorated with stars.
Some mocked others saying: 'You were silent, great
talker,'
Addressing him who never spoke but always listened.
Sodume threw a ball of fire
Displaying flashes of lightning in the distant horizon,
Its flashes making paths in the sky.
Those who like to play sped down on them,
Swinging from ray to ray as they descended to the earth.

Nomkhubulwane: goddess of change & ultimate balance (Zulu
    thought/religion)
Somahle: father of the beautiful days (i.e. festivals & feasts)
Somazwi: knower of words/good at public speaking. Also master of words
    (*Izwi* means a word or voice)
Simo: God assigned the task of maintaining the constancy of change
    (Zulu thought/religion)
Sodume & Nodume: male & female forces descriptive of the two types of
    thunder; one-low, aggressive and threatening; the other high-
    pitched & urgent (Zulu thought system). Sodume means the
    father of the thunder-force. Nodume means the mother of the
    thunder-force. (No-indicates feminine gender & is the

shortened form of *uNina* meaning mother.)(So-indicates masculine gender & is the shortened form of *uyilo* meaning father)—the footnotes are taken directly from Mazisi Kunene's introduction to Anthems of Decades (1981)

IV

The ancestors
& the sacred mountains
(1982)

A heritage of liberation

Since it was you who in all these thin seasons
Gave to our minds the vision of life,
Take these weapons for our children's children.
They were ours.
They broke the enemies' encirclements.
So let our children live with our voices,
With all the abundance of our nightmares.
Let them bury us in the mountain
To remind them of our wanderings.
The sunset steals our youth,
We must depart.
We must follow the trail of the killer-bird
Or else sleep the sleep of terror
To generations hereafter,
May they inherit our dream of the festival,
We who smelt the acrid smell of death,
Who saw the vultures leave our comrade's flesh,
We bequeath to you the rays of the morning…

First day after the war

We heard the songs of a wedding party.
We saw a soft light coiling
Round the young blades of grass.
At first we hesitated, then we saw her footprints.
Her face emerged, then her eyes of freedom!
She woke us up with a smile saying,
'What day is this that comes suddenly?'
We said, 'It is the first day after the war.'
Then without waiting we ran to the open space
Ululating to the mountains and the pathways,
Calling people from all the circles of the earth.
We shook up the old man, demanding a festival.
We asked for all the first fruits of the season.
We held hands with a stranger.
We shouted across the waterfalls.
People came from all lands.
It was the first day of peace.
We saw our Ancestors travelling tall on the horizon.

Journey to the Sacred Mountains

The sun accompanied me
Thrusting its rays over the mountains of Ndini.*
On either side of me, columns of red fire quivered,
Making a corridor of light for my shadow.
The long grass of the hills was bent low
As though to whisper some secret to the earth.
People's shadows walk eternally on earth,
I saw them swirling in the wind,
I laughed and ran by their power,
The Holy Ones spoke and everything was silent;
(All creatures woke from their sleep)
Their voices broke through the waterfalls,
Anthems echoed from the mountains,
They eddied to the horizon like a great wave.
The whole earth was enveloped in their dream.
Those chosen before us showed us the way.
They led us silently to the sacred mountains.
There we listened to the great epics,
We heard the voices of the ancient poets,
We were basking in the legends of our Forefathers,
Certain the child on our back shall grow without fear,
And all things great and beautiful shall follow him.

---

* Proper name. Refer to the poet's explanation on page 11

Phakeni's farewell

(Tribute to Robert Rasha, one of South Africa's greatest political leaders)

Part I

The round calabash overflows with beer,
Crowds assemble before the circular place.
The children peep from the hills like frightened birds.
Voices approach from the low valley,
Voices like the hiss of a gathering storm,
Voices of women, voices of men, voices of children.
In the chaos the ancestral song is heard
Low like a river trapped in a gorge.
Someone weeps uncontrollably.
Someone sings the song in a beat of marching elephants.
Wait! The gorgeous woman with the ancient coiffure –
Who is she?
Who is she who walks into the center?
Crowds retreat from her.
She kneels and tells others to follow her gesture.
She takes out a barbed spear and points to the sun.
Others who know her meanings raise their hands:
Like tails of the sunrays at dawn!
Like a forest of flowers suddenly sprung from a cliff!
Like the hair of the wind shocked by a new spectacle!

Suddenly she puts a round grain basket before them.
With lips opened in awe and wonderment they see:
It is a pumpkin from the garden of Phakeni.
Then the crying, then the singing, then the incantations

Until the whole valley hums like human bees.
These are they who sheltered the sacred truths,
Whose kindness made truth round and desirable,
Who laughed for all things in the universe,
May they prosper and fulfill the promise of the harvest.
There was a man who sat alone
Like time observing a crowd,
Like a roadside boulder watching the evening.
He did not move, only his eyes moved.
Was he the father of Phakeni? Was he the oracle?
Was he some observer from generations to come?
His thunder-force held the whole valley in awe.

But the woman threw her spear against the mountain.
Then flashes of lightning jumped from the sky.
The children of the earth were paralyzed by fear.
Yet not Phakeni.

He strode to and fro,
He spoke as if to fire the crowds with courage!
'Death is not the only thing
It is a lie that flickers only once and is extinguished,
It cannot erase the meaningful acts of humankind.
Then why spend time in morbid gestures?'
He turned away from them to wash his feet in the river,
To stare at the new generations with joy and tears.
Then big drops of rain came and washed away his vision,
A large shield of darkness descended from the sky,
People listened to the stories again,
They slept on their arms against the ground.
They turned their backs from the night.
They made the fierce posture of battle.

Part II

The promise, the failure and the lesson

Your young season was to come with green leaves
To sprout from the earth with voices of the red bird,
Choruses of full moons were to be sung everywhere.
We were to clear the pathway for the new season,
We were to wait for the sign of the rainbow.
You were the promise, you were to lead the festival,
You were to come with two ceremonial spears
To celebrate at the top of the hill,
To celebrate the birth of the sacred twins.

Then disintegration! the season of tears,
Night of darkness, ghost of the sun.
Alone the voice travels to its final point
Desert-dust chases the love-bird to death,
Two sentinels watch the strange grave.
The red sun swims out of the ocean,
The western hills stare at the flying eagle
As though to tell all hereafter
To shout out the night!
To preserve the centric point of our dreams
Despite the menacing clouds of white locusts.

There is a heritage of wisdom in the sky:
The continuous succession of suns, and moons,
The furtherance of love through the soul of the clouds.
The inverted bowl pouring out the abundance of stars,

The fierce encounter of our truth and their truth

The suspended rivers churning out into the sea
The earth, our earth, falling slowly into sleep.
Her eyes closing into the darkness of the rains,
The vision of the green plant in her hand.
The preponderance of her dreams of tomorrow,
The magic awakening of our lives,
The coalescence of our minds beyond the mountain,
The rediscovery of our clansmen,
The long embrace, the tears of joy across the desert!

---

*Phakeni: reference to Robert Resha/seen as a catalyst in the rebirth of
the human race.
*Pointing of spear to the sun: "is a gesture symbolizing Phakeni's
strength, courage and creative energy."
*Sun: "a symbol of life and creativity."
*Rainbow: "promise of a new order after destructive forces."
*Sacred twins: "allusion to the twins who originated from the reed and
started the human family according to Zulu creation myth."
*Pumpkin from the garden of Phakeni: "symbolizes the significant deeds
of Phakeni which sustain and nourish society."

Ecstasy of a song

I am the burning forest
Whose great flames do not cease
Despite the age of the earth.
I wear the blue garments of the sky
I ride a cyclone
I wander freely in the path of light
I pluck the luxuriant plants of dreams
I build a mountain opposite the space of Nohhoyi.
I say: 'Fill the rivers
Fill them with rain
Torment the fools with singing
Sing to the world!'

Sword eulogizing itself after a massacre

By the skills of broken men I was molded,
I reared my head proud of my heritage of steel,
I tore into the bowels of men
And tasted the sweetness of blood.
My appetites were roused,
Again and again I returned to the feast.
To hear the tales of foolish men;
They who boasted their feats of killing.
I lay down and watched their frightened eyes.

I was praised,
I the devourer of a thousand villages;
With reverence they carried me
To boast before the assemblies of men.

Satisfied
They sat down with me
Picking from me the particles of dust
And turning my face to all parts of the earth.
By the terror in their eyes I knew
The shadows of the dead haunted them,
Tearing their minds to the voices of the innocent.

Loneliness of an old man

By the cold light of the night
In the center of a dark house
Your eyes emerged in pursuit of silence;
Of voices that dissolve into nothingness,
Of echoes that float from distant mountains.
The full moon rises beside a hanging cloud.
At the high point it sinks and vanishes,
Perchance it has felt your spreading sadness –
Your memories of youth fall like winter leaves,
This is the eternal cycle of the beginnings.
You are growing into the earth,
You are dying slowly through the final season.

Return of peace

Like a flash of lighting
You run a hundred times to the horizon
And sit by the fireside with the old men,
You listen to their tales of wars,
They ask you:
'What secrets do you bring?
What message is still to be told?
We were to be the last,
We were to sing the great song and die
But you came.
You disturbed our morning,
You interfered with the vision of the final dream.
You said, when our tale has been told
You shall bring a young prophet to sing,
All hail! to the bending face of the flower,
All hail to the seed that is fighting the earth,
All hail to life!'

Return of the Golden Age

We waited for the soft things of dawn
To see the movement of light over the horizon.
From the round hills we heard a sound,
We heard a song thrust into the center of the sky,
We heard the laughter of children.
Each one was like a star shining into the night,
Each one spoke the joy in her eyes.

We saw the palm-tree playing with the cloud,
We heard the poems of the wind.
Dawn came, and hung on a broken house
And put her hands there to rest,
Perhaps to touch with her fingers the growing things.
There are those who are born of the sun
Who by their lips give life to the withered leaf.

But others are the spirit of the forest,
They penetrate the root of the ancient tree
Whose heart beats with the flowing river.
They have gazed into the cave of beginnings
And seen the earth when it was young.
These are wise ones who hold our wisdom.
When all has been uttered they shall speak.

Someone from the past shall touch your shoulder,
Someone whose hands are familiar,
Someone who has said:
We are the fathers of the poet, we shall rise with the sun

And at her zenith sing her songs of the festival
Proclaiming the dividing line of the morning.
The richness of yesterday's season
Shall nourish the thin leaves of the young plant,
All the seasons shall bring the flower
Creating a dazzle of light beside the forest.
For it is here that our affluence first began.

A vision of Zosukuma

With the courage of the sea
I charged into the shores of the earth,
At the end of the white mist
A face, my child, a face of the beautiful sun,
Travelers wait for him.
They come from the four directions of the earth,
From this center there is a winding path,
Long stems of flowers hang over the earth,
They swell with the seed of the new year.
My child takes the poem that is old
And learns from it our own legends
To see life with the eyes of the Forefathers.
For all creatures have their way of finding a home,
Like the hunting dog, like the stampeding elephant,
Like us who have found a moving mountain.

Death of the miners or the widows of the earth

We waited in silence for our children.
Their voices wounded the earth.
It was as if our very footsteps
Crushed their last breath of life.

The final day came...
Our village was a forest of new comers and goers,
Decorations were suspended on high poles of the village.
Men with polished shoes and women with high-pitched voices
Paraded the streets like some freshly fed peacocks.
Yes! Bells, voices, sirens:
'THE LEADER has arrived'
Proclaimed the carefully woven banners.
Only then and only then did we know the fate of our men...

Life continues unchanged in our village.
Men still leave early at dawn.
Silence walks where once was the pomp of yesterday.
Old tattered flags hang on the side-streets.
Only we and the memory of pain remain.
We are the widows of the earth,
We are the orphans of stone,
Insanity stares unblinkingly through the broken windows.

Those who waited in the night of the earth
Until their eyes succumbed to the darkness,
Until they bellowed with mocking laughter,
Until they lived the illusion of escape--
They were our fathers, our husbands and our children.

On that day, on that morning
The last words were spoken softly on the doorsteps,
The air was cold,
The farewells were long.

News travels fast these days,
Suddenly our village was invaded by whiskered men,
By those who spoke for us to yet others
Who spoke for us.
They clucked in a language that was foreign to us.

These were Publicmen and writers
And men of substance who make money and interviews.
Some spoke casually to us
Until told we were the wives and children of 'Them'.

Then they came closer to us to dissect our feelings,
To know how we had spent the night.

They did not remember
We had seen them that very day
Talking wisely for us in those boxes.
From their words you would have thought
They know all the buried truths of our husbands' terrors.
In truth to know so much is a gift of divining.

World wisdom

Great thoughts have penetrated into the ground
To be nourished by time and silent movements
No one should stop here till the season has passed
No one must break the bead of the storm
Until the eyes are worn out with seeing
Like tattered rags.
What will come last will be the truth
Since the beating of the heart outlasts
The nakedness of the bones.
Yes, in time we shall grow wise
And cross the Bramaputra,[*] the Nile and the Amazon
Reaping from there the wisdom of our earth.

---

[*] One of the world's largest river located near Dhubri, India. Also connects through the far eastern state of Arunachal Pradesh. Historically has its connection from to Tibet.

Progress

The madman has entered our house with violence
Defiling our sacred grounds
Claiming the single truth of the universe,
Bending down our high priests with iron
Ah! Yes, the children,
Who walked on our Forefathers' graves
Shall be stricken with madness.
They shall grow the fangs of the lizard,
They shall devour each other before our eyes
And by an ancient command
It is forbidden for us to stop them!

At the seashore

Empty shells, black stones, seashore,
Witness against the blue sky;
Mother of the red sand and white tails of oceans.
'Follow me' I said to the little crabs and they did.
Now we possess the whole wide world--
The soft things of water, the holes, the sea plants
The ability to see the green stones.
We are the breed awaited these thousand years,
We don't need a dream, we don't need a paradise,
We are the dream, the crossway of the rainbow,
The dawn that breaks all round the earth.
We shall plant motherhood on all things
And through us the season shall see the world's
awakening...

Encounter with the ancestors

If by chance we come across those who are old,
Who have seen into the heart of the night,
We must not flee in terror of their secrets
But watch their eyes slowly reveal the chameleon.
We must follow the direction of their little finger
Where begins the story, the beginning of seeing.
Our guide through the desert must sing then,
Making our minds break the web of light
To create a new path of wisdom.
The child who is born from this vision
Shall be the envy of her age.
She must plant the first season of a million years.
If her sun seems too small at first,
It is only the circle breaking the seed.
Those who watch the birth of things
See only the flower in the womb of the calabash
Where all wisdom is stored.
They shall bend down beside the quiet river
To quench the thirst of the desert.
Yet hunger alone does not make one an oracle,
It nourishes insanity and people get thin.
But both water and fruit enrich the mind,
For only through laughter are we made human,
Only thus are we guided through to the Forefathers' epics.

Journey into universal wisdom

One day I'll find you at broad daylight.
I'll take you away from them
And walk with you until we disappear into the darkness,
Until we are enveloped by the night.
There, I'll show you the beginnings of a new earth,
I'll teach you the new birth-movements,
Letting you imitate these great ecstasies.
I'll show you a vast ocean below
Where strange creatures emerge.
You will hear them speak in their own language.
By your own dream
You shall inherit their truth,
Making it nourish yours and all your children.
I shall lead you into the valley of tranquility
Where you shall learn the anthems of the universe.
To speak finally the secret languages of the cosmos.

Mathabo

Then the stranger has found his place of rest:
Your pure springs with showers of rain
And reeds on the river-bed, with green sunshine.
He whom you have led by the hand is here.
His head reaches the skies and his eyes into the star.
'Pride of our House, giraffe of my Forefathers,
Unending river of ecstatic milk,
Prove to me you are neither man nor woman but a god
Whose rich creations are eternal growth.
Tell me when I see you: "I have nourished his mind,
I have filled it with plants and yellow flowers."
Give me the sacred movements
Plant the tree of the monkey.'
You are born of the mists and of the dream.
Do not move, do not disturb the eternal cycles
But weave into them the sacred knots of the rainbow
And the generations that are to come must sing.

A meeting with Vilakazi, the great Zulu poet

Sleep tried to split us apart
But the great dream created a new sun.
Through its towering rays two worlds emerged
And our twin planets opened to each other.
I saw you descending from a dazzling hill,
Your presence filled the whole world.
I heard the drum beat behind your footsteps
And the children of the south began to sing.
They walked on the ancient path of the goddess
Nomkhubulwane[*]
And the old dancing arena was filled with festival crowds.
Your great songs echoed to the accompaniment of the
festival horn.
It was the beginning of our ancient new year
Before the foreigners came, before they planted their own
emblems.
I came to the arena and you held my hand.
Together we danced the boast-dance of our forefathers,
We sang the great anthems of the uLundi[*] mountains.

---

[*] uLundi is a place in Durban, South Africa/Also the site of the final
battle of the Anglo-Zulu war
[*]Nomkhubulwane: daughter of God & goddess of balance (Zulu thought
system)
This reference affirms Kunene's avowal in his introduction to his poetry
book, Anthem of Decades, that Nomkhubulwane is responsible as
creative force since the "creative purpose is both physical and spiritual.

To Tu Fu, Beethoven, Va Dong, Magolwane and all the great poets of humankind

The great mountain trembles from your song.
The varied paths of the Mkize* clan have opened.
Beautiful son of Nomkhubulwane*,
You ate the black fruits of thunder
And cleaved the forest like an afternoon sun.
You pierced the blankets of clouds with the voice of
A singing bird.
You led the traveler to the alcoves of paradise.
There, people fed their minds with fresh memories,
Praising your greatness, they proclaimed:
'Bull of many folds, who comes and goes at will,
Lick the young calf with the soft end of your tongue.
Make its fantasies linger at the place of meeting.
Make the wise witness the fearful creations.
When they climb the sacred mountain,
May they boast your name.
In that moment, give them power to listen.

---

* Mkize: Clan in Zululand
* Nomkhubulwane: daughter of God/manifestation of God's creative
  power (Zulu mythology)
* Magolwane: Shaka's court poet. Renowned for revolutionizing Zulu
  poetry

Then swirling like a hurricane,
Scatter the dew on the fields and over the forest.
Hold the round clay-pot over their heads
Until they declare:
"Come with us, you, who are proud,
Grant immortality to all things,
Give life to the wise and the restless children,
Grant the freedoms promised to us these thousand years ago."

When my poems were lost

Where is the arbiter of a thousand languages?
Where is the narrator of the traveler's tales?
Where is the hunter of the beautiful words?
Where is the patient one whose visions are the stars?
Where is the magic lover whose hands carry the season's
 secrets?
Where is the stranger who walked through the mist?
Where is the granddaughter of the first sea-mountains?
Where is the one who created a feast of song in the
wilderness?
Where is the one who gave milk to the children?
Where is the one who no longer sang the songs of the
birds?
Where is the one whose hair was white like the waterfalls?

Unfinished epic

For the truth must outlast the prophet
And those who follow must bow down to this moment,
Choosing a place where to praise his mind.
Yet words are thieves that lull the watchman,
They seize the resting place of the eternal truths,
They take the garden for the violent seed.
We are deceived by them and through them
We imagine a greater poet than was ever born.
Yet we must curse you for the unfinished journey.
Because of you a flock of vultures threatens us.
Had you, by your wisdom, narrated the whole tale
Our children's children would have been spared the
 humiliation.

Vision of Nomkhubulwane

The round ball of the mist hangs over the mountain,
Nomkhubulwane* the goddess has touched the center,
Breaking it in the four directions of the earth.
She is the white cloud veiled in crimson.
With footsteps as gentle as the movement of water
She follows the round stones and the young plant.

From the river her shadow rises against the hill
And the curled wave tosses the ripe fruit,
The small creatures of the earth declare a festival.
A swift movement of the wind, rich with red scents,
Fills the valley of Nomangei.
Voices rise in the horizon, people are shouting,
They bring the beautiful dream to our earth.

From the furthest depths of the ocean
The celebration of her season is heard
And the creatures of the forest come running,
The children of the earth sit in a semi-circle,
The gourds in their hands are filled with wisdom.

---

* Nomkhubulwane: daughter of God/manifestation of God's creative
  purpose (Zulu mythology)
*Nomagei: Valley in a place known as Nomangei
* Gourd: calabash/bottle made from the dried shell of a bottle gourd

V

*Echoes from
the mountain*

Playful words of childhood

I shall not anymore forebear to enter into the womb of the earth
So long as I know from it, I have the gift of a promise to escape,
As long as I know what exists exists forever and ever,
What has existed shall exist and exist again and again,
This is the sacred vow of life.
Eternal movement is eternal birth,
Thus the meaning is enshrined in the mind of our eternal sun,
There always shall be images of life and its echoes.
There reside in all minds sounds of our dances.
The mind possesses the seeds of future times and eternity,
The mind replays its own birth forever and ever.
There is foolishness that claims that we shall end.
And behind us there shall only be deserts!
But this is only an image induced by a falling tree,
A tree that grows until it curls and dies.
And yet our tomorrows' truths are images of eternity.
A cloud is circular and predicts the essence of the earth.
Thus it assumes the quality of Being.
A cloud eternally predicts the fate of our earth.
This power shall ultimately breathe itself into eternity!
And yet all things begin as a dream
And all growing and growth shall multiply.
Life inhabits a vast space without end.
We must not be swallowed in the fears of crowding and death.

A fear of death is the fear of the mother of the sun.
The sun has always accompanied us by her emergence of
its creative fruit.
The creative fruit is foretold by the emergence of the
varied mushrooms
From the earth I shall respond to you, Great Mother of
Eternity!
You, who nourishes your children from a single vessel,
You, who are endowed with four breasts, give us the
echoes of your song;
Yet at last I have found you mother of the African Twins
You who feed us from the left and right breasts, grant us
fullness of life.
Great Mother, who are beautiful even in your tender feet,
You gave birth to all the children of the earth,
You stared in amazement counting and humming with us
like bees,
You, who are beautiful even when wrinkled with age,
You are growing young even from your own tales of
immortality,
You emerged with your youth woven into your own
beautiful legends,
The legends that abound with laughter.
They say you do not age, age is only a shell encasing our
lives.
It is an ancient basket encasing our being.
We, your progeny, patiently shall create and create your
songs
To enrich our own tales of love, of loving!

The plaiting of the mind

Whatever you shall do, you shall do to imitate the mind
Although I am still just a child, I shall imitate your eternal
rays of light
Yet my hands are still soft, they shall follow you into your
destiny
Thus as I grow older my hands will enter into the images of
your being
Your mind is patient and deep and generous
Suddenly it may enter your cycle and be born into our
moments of perfection
Your knots will demand to be woven twice, and be perfect
and be of a woman
So that we may realize that our hands are not hands
But images of the mind to which we must listen
To listen to the long command, a long command of time
from within
Her speed had flourished through her ability to rule
And in turn, through her power, we have succumbed!
We shall pretend to be overcome by her through weakness
But we know this way we shall create and create again all
the knots of eternity like the plaited hair of our young
children who dance with the moon.
Pliant they seem to be as if, they would suddenly snap
But not so, they only slip away from the carelessness of our
fingers
All this shall happen before our very eyes
In which the smallest things will enter the wind to create

the universe
The universe that is vast and endless.
Thus everything shall be born of the other.
All things and all generations at the festival,
Shall know their dance-movements!
They all shall know how to enter
And how to escape the crippling dialogues of time!
Great powers do not rely on our powers, but on the powers
of creation
Yet in the skills that created us there are paths to lead us
to escape
The needle chooses its moment of retreat
And when the fingers resist the moments of retreat
Others following shall add other sacred movements
And in them they shall dictate the moments of creation
Thus Thandiwe is singing her song
Commanding some, and commanding others to create a
space to escape
And the mind shall thus be commanded to spin her
movements of retreat

So that...

So that we may be wise
Wise beyond the limits of our wisdom
We must walk firmly on the sacred earth;
Despite our tender soft feet, which are challenged by
fragments of broken stones
We must trample on the sharp edges of the crude boulders
And yet we must still persist on the cruel gravel.
Our feet must not be hard and stubborn against the earth
But let it not be hardness of the hoofs of the stampeding
giraffes
Whose memory of the earth is lost on the hardened
ground
But may it be our feet that recall the pain and joy
They must eternally recall the fear of pursuing the truths
Thus the mind shall replay the memory of pain
Encased in the child's fear we must always remember the
earth
And constantly share the violence of the earth
Remembering always the sacred moment of our awakening
And simultaneously inherit the folly of our own violence
And thus be endowed with the power of awakening
We shall carry the child on our backs
A child who will teach us and in turn we shall teach her
from the emerging suns
Such acts of teaching are acts of knowing
But the acts of knowing are our burdens
So blessed is the one who is not afraid of carrying the earth
And carries the earth on his back and on his head

Thus greatness is of dual meanings as knowledge is dual
Intellect is old, great intellect is trapped in childhood
Thus true genius must not cease to grow backwards.
Such was the command of our Ancestors.
Yet the wisdom of foreigners is one-sided
It is cleverness of counting and the mind of iron.
We who are old know that Humanity is endowed with two minds;
The mind that is soft like the body of a python
The mind that is hard like an old log.
Thus the child is endowed with worlds, worlds that desire
The child is us as we dance in the open space.
Yet the child is not a child but an adult
And is an old man devoid of a bead.
Yet when we entrap him with fears he is a child
The mind is like a tender tree that bends easily
Yet the tree is old and hard and has its beginning from generations
As we grow we are old
Since all that grows emerges from fantasy!

Africa's celebration of freedom

From our very sacred moments, we uttered these words
We vowed that the vast forests shall follow us
The vast jungles shall speak to us
They shall sing the songs that are locked into their power
Their voices shall echo into the tumbling waves
We too must follow these movements of water
Singing and shouting our songs from the ends of the earth
Our voices will explode from the razor sharp rocks of the
South
They that will face the sky with their power
The rivers shall gallop widely back to their homes.
No longer shall we be postured in suspense
As though we were ready to turn back
To turn back to the swirling waves in circles
Following the path that will carry them into the womb of
time
Forced then to pretend the postures of heroes at war.
It is the lone hero who shall carve our paths!
Yes the power of the rains has triumphed
To be heard again and again
From the center of the earth that is with us.
Now, the earth is bursting with our voices
Voices that are held in suspense over our homes and in the
wilderness
Our zone of the earth is conscious of our power!
It has allowed us sing the anthem of awakening

And let us sing too our long lost melodies
We guessed our victories as we entered our continent
Yet for now we have only seen the long lost flashes of lightning
The flashes of lightning that sealed our paths and those of the earth
Our drums have created the echoes of the mountains!
The great river is the returning home to the eternal ocean!

In celebration of our sun

The night has fallen.
We were overwhelmed by night as it descended on us.
This was a sign that was to seize our earth.
The sun has nourished our minds
The sun has refused to challenge us with defeat.
On that moment we returned silently into our mother's womb,
We were in terror of the nights that were collapsing before us.
It was at that moment that we could see clearly our sacred flame
We were lifted through our dreams.
Finally! we felt as if we had entered our morning
Our tired feet had walked without stopping into foreign lands
We had escaped through, with our restless spirits!
Now we stand on the brink of eternity, guessing all truths,
The truths that we shall never know.
Only our knowing shall beset us with images of our ignorance!
All these challenges have tested our powers of knowing
We have entered the state of infancy.
We are infants before they have touched the cords of their birth.
Suddenly we have awoken to the aura of our own eternal powers.
Such power is of the child that constantly suckles at its fingers!

Yet all these happenings await the instance of our sacred sun,
The sun is the guardian of all life,
It is the sun that, by its power, has led us to the morning.
We are at the arena of our sacred dances,
We shall celebrate our morning with our song that is born of the sun!
Our paths are open in all directions, and our sun embraces all suns!
Our dances are open to all passersby and into the pathways of the sun.
Yes, the sun is older than we, the sun is more beautiful than we!
It came into being before we were born.
Our elders have told us this story, before we were misled by our own ignorance.
It is because of you that I have emerged suddenly,
I have emerged from my blindness.
Yet it was you who stirred for me the drop of water
Such glitter shone violently into me from the desert.
And through you, all the creatures of the wilderness are assembled
To drink from your finger!
They were nourished and people were fulfilled.
Not from the abundance of our Southern springs
Where the sacred springs of the South are controlled,

But from their thirst that challenged us through our nothingness.
You followed me through the forest
And said I must come to feed the orphans of the earth.
At first I hesitated, since my breasts were devoid of their

nourishment.
But you cautioned me and said
It is not from the fullness of my breasts that we are nourished,
But from the acts that elevate our bonds
Our spirits shall spring from the warmth of our sun.
Our sun is old, it is nourished by the powers that are hidden from all humanity.
Alas it is we who are the source of the abundance.
Frequently we are fulfilled beyond our powers of knowing
Such extravagance has overwhelmed all our beginnings.
Such beginnings spring from our long forgotten wounds
To stay till the end of time, counting the flashes of our existence.
It is these powers that made us supersede our sense of being.
Humanity thus is misled from its essence of life on earth.
Because of you, I have awakened from a long sleep.
I too have reason to cast away my sacred staff,
That staff that has accompanied me on my path since before I was born.
From all angles I search for my blindness
I have lost my power to see,
For those who cannot see surrender their ability to dance in public!

And the one

And the one whom I must love
Must reciprocate and reciprocate through loving.
Simultaneously I shall face the terror of loving in silence
Lest I may love her whose love is weak.
I may be injured and experience pain
In the open space I shall be exposed.
Endless boulders shall be hurled at me.
To escape I must tie a strong knot
And encircle myself around my waist
To imprison myself into those moments of loving.
I shall be freed by power that is mine
To allow it to escape into the sun, at will, from me.
Thus I shall not experience the pain,
But from her, who has loved me, gain my freedom.
Finally I shall experience the warmth of her embrace,
Finally someone must command me to open my hands,
To open the palm of my hand to reveal my secrets,
The secret movements through which I must travel.
I shall open my soft hands to expose my myriad baths
Through the sacred paths of my return that are open to
me.
Forever and ever I shall watch my enemies fall into decay.
Nothing shall be new nor will it be celebrated.
From underneath new lines shall emerge,
Those sacred lines shall be soft and delicate,
In that moment we shall begin again a new season,
A new season of loving to which we shall dance the dance

of the ram.
The ancient ram shall begin to teach its young the art of
falling.
Triumphantly again and again as we return and walk the
earth,
We shall walk the earth until the earth is soft like an early
summer plant;
It shall emerge slowly until it attains the warmth of our
friendship.

The fading flower

It is your fault my beautiful flower you have withered
On this bright day, on this violent day.
You made fun of us as you curled into your womb,
As you curled eternally into the mysteries of your
beginnings.
Then I could not experience your moment of perfection.
I had been made to create for us an image from the
shadows of yesteryears.
Yet your greatness is to be fulfilled!
But I know you my flower, you are the messenger of my
beauty
You are the perfection in-between times as you reveal your
image
You are beautiful as you yearn to be perfect.
You must believe in things unfolding and changing.
Time must yet give birth to a billion billion years,
Yet there are others that may still be born, those that are
still to be born.
And yet when all the stars have disappeared,
There will be rampant curse of all things falling into the
night.
People will be seduced by the fierce clouds of darkness,
The earth itself will be immersed in fears of annihilation.
Again and again the infant shall be terrorized by the
healer;
The healer must search, must search for the truth, in
between the stars.
From this zone, often images of life emerge from other

worlds.

The healer must console the child for such is the role of the parent.

A parent must cure even in these times of folly,

Even when the parent knows this will pass.

The awakening of the minds

So it shall be when I shall be on the verge of insanity.
You shall accompany me, you who is insane.
And in that state of mindlessness I shall enter deep into insanity
So that I too can acquire the terrors of your madness.
And in that state of madness I shall go deep into insanity.
My deeds will be the spectacle that shall observe my emerging,
Watching me, and through their minds celebrating my movements.
Yes, I shall not be alone but with a multitude of selves in the womb.
They shall direct me not to commit acts of madness
Lest I be expelled from the congregation of the insane
Lest I may suddenly find the old ladies sacred tooth missing.
Yet humanity must speak with its tongue
With its lips, its teeth, all in act of oneness.
I request you, who is wise, to accompany me.
Do not hesitate before I complete my journey.
I must not flatter myself into an instance of nothingness
And be plunged into things that devoid of movement
Lest through them I may encounter hollow pillars for holding.
Give me, then, your power to keep anchored on the earth.
Let it be the power of the mind and be of the mind only.
Let these powers be beyond my thirteenth margin,
So that they may manifest themselves on the desirable

paths of madness.

This way we shall be assured that we are no more alone.

But we are possessed with an abundance of our powers of awakening.

Such powers were buried in the secret chambers of our minds.

And when these thoughts emerge, humanity will awake again suddenly!

Humanity shall clap its hands in amazement,

Surprised that the center that was missing has returned!

Yet what was missing is the power of the mind but not of life.

Yet all madness is the disturbance of the mind

And some of its acts are of the awakening of the mind.

It is yet the awakening of a million million minds

To celebrate the awakening of humanity.